D1117510

Language Builders

Iris and Ian Learn about
INTERJECTIONS

by Darice Bailer
illustrated by Kelsey Oseid

Content Consultant
Roxanne Owens
Associate Professor, Elementary Reading
DePaul University

ESSAMINE COUNTY PUBLIC LIBRARY
600 SOUTH MAIN STREET
NICHOLASVILLE, KY 40356
(859) 885-3523

NORWOOD HOUSE PRESS
CHICAGO, ILLINOIS

Norwood House Press
P.O. Box 316598
Chicago, Illinois 60631
For information regarding Norwood House Press, please visit
our website at:
www.norwoodhousepress.com or call 866-565-2900.

Editor: Melissa York
Designer: Jake Nordby
Project Management: Red Line Editorial

Library of Congress Cataloging-in-Publication Data
Bailer, Darice, author.
 Iris and Ian learn about interjections / By Darice Bailer ;
Illustrated by Kelsey Oseid.
      p. cm. -- (Language Builders)
 Includes bibliographical references.
 Summary: "While writing stories, Iris and Ian learn how
to use interjections. Concepts include: basic definition and
usage of interjections; exclamation points; interjections in
dialogue; multiword interjections; onomatopoeia; and other
parts of speech used as interjections. Activities in the back
help reinforce text concepts. Includes glossary and additional
resources"-- Provided by publisher.
 Audience: Ages: 7-10
 ISBN 978-1-59953-672-9 (library edition : alk. paper) -- ISBN
978-1-60357-732-8 (ebook)
 1. English language--Interjections--Juvenile literature. 2.
English language--Parts of speech--Juvenile literature. I. Oseid,
Kelsey, illustrator. II. Title.
 PE1355.B35 2015
 428.1--dc22

                                2014030268

©2015 by Norwood House Press.
All rights reserved.
No part of this book may be reproduced without written
permission from the publisher.
Manufactured in the United States of America in North
Mankato, Minnesota.
262N—122014

Words in **black bold** are defined in the glossary.

Exciting Interjections

Yikes! What is Mrs. Green up to? She was acting really weird in school today. She's talking like a kid! When Ian got all his math problems right, she held up his paper and said, "Awesome!" And when I told Mrs. Green I'm going to be Annie in the school play, she said, "Cool!"

Mrs. Green used words like that all day long. She said she was using **interjections**. They're usually one or two words that show **emotion** and shout out how you feel. Interjections can show happiness. "Yippee!" Or excitement. "Hooray!" Or surprise. "Wow!"

Mrs. Green said we should use interjections in our writing. Seriously? Talk like that in a story? Mrs. Green also gave us a riddle to solve. She said, "What makes a point with interjections?" Whoa! What does Mrs. Green's riddle mean? Well, my buddy Ian will know. I'll ask him on the playground at recess.

Brilliant!
By Iris, age 8

Hooray! It was finally lunchtime. The smell of chicken tacos floated down the hall. Ian gripped his lunch tray and looked around the noisy cafeteria. Hey! There was Iris. Ian slid his red tray onto the table and sat down. "Hi," he said. Iris held her head in her hands.

"Hey, Iris! Don't you like chicken tacos?" Ian bit into the crunchy taco and looked at her.

"How can you eat tacos when we have to write our funny stories this afternoon!" Iris ran her fingers through her hair. "I'm doomed! Doomed! Doomed!"

"Why are you doomed?" asked Ian.

"My story is an enormous disaster. I'm going to get kicked out of third grade and sent to summer school in the Everglades. There will be alligators on the playground. Oh, why did I ever leave second grade?"

Good grief! Ian thought. All this fuss about writing? "You mean you're worried about the funny story Mrs. Green wants us to write called *Help! Mrs. Green put me in charge. Class 3-G is driving me crazy*!"

"Yes, that one!" Iris said. "And the writing is driving me crazy! I can't write. My stories are always boring! Ugh!"

Ian laughed. "Iris! All you have to do is write the way you talk!"

Iris stared at him. "That's funny. Mrs. Green keeps telling us to spice up our writing with interjections!"

Iris thought about what Mrs. Green had taught them about interjections. "Interjections are **exclamations**," she remembered. "They usually come at the beginning of a sentence. But sometimes they come in the middle."

"Yes," Ian agreed. "Interjections shout! They scream out whether you're sad, mad, or glad. Interjections show your feelings. You love to do that, Iris. Just sprinkle interjections in your story and your words will sing."

The two children ate their chicken tacos and carrot sticks and emptied their trays. Then they lined up with the rest of the class by the door to the playground. Outside, Iris raced Ian across the grass from one end of the playground to the other. "Hooray!" Iris said.

Ian leaned over, resting his hands on his knees. "Wow, you're fast," he said, catching his breath. "Hey, we just used two interjections. When you shouted *hooray*, you said you were happy you beat me. I said *wow* to show my surprise at how fast you ran. *Hooray* and *wow* are two words you can use in your story."

"Oh, my gosh! You're right." Iris laughed. "And *oh, my gosh* is an interjection, too." Mrs. Green taught the children that interjections are usually one or two words. But sometimes they can be three like "Out of sight!" or "Ooh-la-la!" Interjections can be whole sentences all by themselves, like "Run!"

"We can work on our stories after school together," Ian said.

Iris dug her purple sneaker into the grass. "Cool! I just wish we could figure out Mrs. Green's riddle. She asked what makes a point with interjections. What do you think she means?"

"Eh," Ian shrugged his shoulders. "I'm sure we'll find out sooner or later."

Iris laughed and waved her pointer finger. "And *eh* is another interjection, Ian! Woo-hoo!"

"Woo-hoo!" Ian laughed. "That is, too!"

That afternoon, the kids rode the bus to Iris's house together. Ian put the finishing touches on his story on the bus. When they got to Iris's house, they sat down in her living room to do homework. Iris pulled her story out of her writing folder and showed Ian what she had so far.

Help! Mrs. Green Put Me in Charge.
Class 3-G Is Driving Me Crazy!
Mrs. Green said she had to go to a meeting. She needed someone to teach the class. She picked me. The kids weren't happy. They talked and talked. They ran around the room. They drove me crazy.

"What do you think so far?" Iris asked.

"Yikes!" Ian said, and frowned. "This doesn't sound like you. First of all, you're not talking, and you're always gabbing. Where's the **dialogue**? Dialogue is conversation. It's what you and other people are saying. Dialogue makes writing more exciting."

"Hmm," Iris said. "Mrs. Green did say that interjections are often used in conversation."

"Remember to use quotation marks to show that someone's talking. You need to capitalize the first word in the sentence, too," said Ian.

"Right!" grinned Iris.

"Sometimes people use interjections when they don't know what to say," Ian added.

"Yes," agreed Iris. "So if, ah, I don't know what to say, I, um, fill up the pauses with interjections."

"So what would Mrs. Green say when she tells you she has to leave class?" Ian asked.

Ha! Iris knew the answer to Ian's question. Two of Mrs. Green's favorite words were "Oh, dear!" And "Oh, dear!" was an interjection!

Iris wrote "Oh, dear!" on her paper. Then she tapped the eraser against her cheek, thinking.

Ian gave her another question to think about. "If Mrs. Green did put you in charge of our class, like a real teacher, what would you think?"

Iris looked at him and started smiling. "Holy cow!"

"Right!" Ian said excitedly.

Iris wrote down *holy cow* and more.
She underlined all the interjections
she used.

"<u>Oh dear!</u>" Mrs. Green said. "I have to go to a meeting today!" Mrs. Green turned and looked at me. "I need someone to teach the class! And Iris, I'd like it to be you!"

<u>Hey</u>, wait a minute. Mrs. Green picked me? I'm only an 8-year-old! <u>Holy cow!</u> I slid down in my chair. I wanted to hide in my desk. But when Mrs. Green left, I was in charge! I told the class to take out a book. "<u>Eww!</u> Do we have to?" Rachel asked.

"The **exclamation points** show where the story is exciting," explained Iris.

"Right," agreed Ian. "But exclamation points do not always follow an interjection. When the story said, 'I need someone to teach the class! And Iris, I'd like it to be you!' there were no interjections."

Iris paused, thinking about everything Mrs. Green taught her. She said out loud, "Interjections can also be different parts of speech."

Ian agreed. "Like **adjectives** describing a good idea. *Brilliant!* Or a **verb**. *Hide!*"

"Yes, the difference is how the word is used. *Nice!* can be an interjection, but in the sentence 'I have a nice friend,' *nice* is an adjective," added Iris.

Ian was getting excited. He stood up and paced around the room as he talked. "But there's more! Interjections can say hello. *Yoo-hoo!* Or good-bye. *Toodle-loo!* They can even be **onomatopoeia** and make sounds. *Ding! Ding!* or *Ow!* or *Zap!*"

"Ah-ha!" exclaimed Iris.

Iris picked up her pencil again.

She underlined the interjections she used.

<u>Oh, my gosh!</u> The kids talked and talked. Jack shot a little eraser across the desks. <u>Zap!</u> The eraser hit Ian in the head. "<u>Ouch!</u>" Ian said. "<u>That hurt!</u>"

Rachel told Jack, "<u>Run!</u>" Then all the kids ran around the desks.

<u>Yikes!</u> What am I going to do? Class 3-G is driving me crazy!

"Could you all, <u>um</u>, just sit down?" I asked. "No!" the class said together.

Mrs. Green seemed to be gone forever. Finally she returned. I wanted to say, "<u>Cool!</u>" Instead, I said, "<u>Phew!</u>"

Iris added an exclamation point to the last word in her story. Then she sat up straight. She waved her pencil in the air. "Hey, wait a minute," she cried. "That's the answer to Mrs. Green's riddle."

"What is?" asked Ian.

Iris explained, "Interjections usually begin sentences: 'Hey' in 'Hey, who shot that paper airplane!'"

"Or 'Wow' in 'Wow, this is really cool!'" added Ian.

"Yes!" continued Iris. "We just use a comma after those interjections. The comma means the feeling isn't quite as strong. But when we want to show a lot of excitement, we add an exclamation point. That's what Mrs. Green meant when she asked us what makes a point. That's the answer to Mrs. Green's riddle!"

"You mean . . ."

"Yes! Mrs. Green meant *don't forget the exclamation point!*"

Ian grinned. "Awesome!" he said.

Know Your Interjections

Interjections show emotion. Happy, sad, bored, excited—interjections can communicate all these feelings. Interjections can say hello and good-bye, or just make silly sounds. Quack!

Interjections are separate from the other words in a sentence, or they stand alone outside of a sentence. An interjection is often followed by an exclamation point. At the beginning or in the middle of a sentence, a comma can follow the interjection instead. Other parts of speech, like adjectives and verbs, can work like interjections, too. But watch out. Not every sentence with an exclamation point has an interjection!

Look back at Iris's letter on page 3. How many interjections can you find there?

Writing Activity

How many interjections can you think of? Can you come up with one for each letter of the alphabet?

When you're done, fill in this silly poem with some of your interjections! How do your interjections add a little zing to this verse?

_____! There's a crocodile, and he's snoring in my bed.

_____! Now he's up, and he bumped his head!

"_____!" said my sister.
"_____!" said my dad.

"_____! Call the zoo right now!" I said.

Glossary

adjectives: words that describe a noun or pronoun.

dialogue: conversation.

emotion: a strong feeling such as love, joy, or sadness.

exclamation points: punctuation marks used to show strong feelings.

exclamations: words said suddenly with emotion.

interjections: words that show emotion.

onomatopoeia: a word that imitates a sound like bzzz or ding-a-ling.

verb: a word that shows action (like run, jump) or being (am, have).

For More Information

Books

Cleary, Brian P. *Cool! Whoa! Ah and Oh! What is an Interjection?* Minneapolis, MN: Millbrook Press, 2013.

McClarnon, Marciann. *Painless Junior Grammar*. Hauppauge, NY: Barron's Educational Series, 2007.

Preciado, Tony, and Rhode Montijo. *Super Grammar*. New York: Scholastic, 2012.

Websites

Schoolhouse Rock
https://www.youtube.com/watch?v=YkAX7Vk3JEw

This funny musical cartoon teaches how interjections are used and gives many examples.

Englishlinx
http://englishlinx.com/interjections/

On this website you can find free worksheets to print out. Use them to practice writing interjections.

About the Author

Darice Bailer has written many books for children. When she was in elementary school she dreamed of becoming a writer.